MW00413546

40 days of
GREATNESS

40 days of
GREATNESS

By Matthew Oliver

Copyright 2015 - Matthew Oliver

Contents

Introduction..................................... 7

HOPE.. 16
STRENGTH...................................... 18
VISION.. 20
MORE.. 22
GREATNESS.................................... 24
JOY... 26
ADVANCE....................................... 28
NEW.. 30
WHOLENESS................................... 32
RESTORATION................................ 34
REVIVAL.. 36
PEACE... 38
REFRESHING.................................. 40
RIGHTEOUSNESS............................ 42
LOVE... 44
LIFE.. 46
WONDERS....................................... 48
LAUGHTER..................................... 50
FORGIVENESS................................. 52
GROWTH.. 54
FAVOR.. 56
POWER... 58
AWE.. 60
REDEMPTION................................. 62
HEALING.. 64

WAR... 66

VICTORY..................................... 68

BREAKTHROUGH.............. 70

EXTRAVAGANT LOVE... 72

CREATIVITY............................ 74

GOODNESS............................ 76

SALVATION............................. 78

FAITHFULNESS.................... 80

CHOSEN.................................... 82

REFRESHING......................... 84

MINE... 86

ABUNDANCE......................... 88

GLORY.. 90

JUSTICE..................................... 92

CELEBRATION...................... 94

You are GREAT

40 Days of Great

Take a moment and think of Greatness. What is the first thought that comes to mind? Was it a person, a moment, a figure? Was it God? Maybe it was a time in your life that was memorable: perhaps a birth or a wedding. Or, **maybe it was something of historical significance:** winning a war, walking on the moon, the right person elected to office.

For you, Greatness may be more about innovation, such as the invention of the car, the I-Phone, or the computer. Others may think of greatness as risking big; stepping out boldly in areas that no one has ever stepped out in before. Still others may think of Greatness as simply immeasurable vastness. Then there is God's Greatness: Great because He is. God holds all things in His hands, both immeasurable and limitless. He is creator and inventor, timeless, uncontainable, and yet personal. There is no one like Him.

After reading this list, you may have come up with your own ideas of Greatness. When you were thinking of Greatness, did you think of YOU? Not what you have done, accomplished, or even achieved. Just you: in your messiness, imperfection and distractions, on your good days and bad, in your successes and failures. You!

The problem we face with understanding Greatness is that we have been programmed to think that Greatness is something achieved, won, or earned. However, if Greatness is a thing, a moment, or an achievement that can be obtained, then the opposite is true as well, Greatness can be lost. Achieving Greatness can become something we have done: I was great at my job, my project was great, that event was a great event. We say, so-and-so was a great leader, a great commander, officer; or the way they handled that situation was great.

When we look at God, we do not see His Greatness limited to a function or an ability, it is not contained in a moment or a time. Greatness is who He is. What does the Bible say about God's Greatness?

Jeremiah 10:6

"There is none like You, O LORD; You are great, and great is Your name in might."

Psalm 96:4

"For great is the LORD and greatly to be praised; He is to be feared above all gods."

1 Chronicles 29:11

"Yours, O LORD, is the greatness and the power and the glory and the victory and the majesty, indeed everything that is in the heavens and the earth; Yours is the dominion, O LORD, and You exalt Yourself as head over all."

Our God is great. These and other numerous scriptures list and help define the Greatness of our God. These definitions do not try to limit His Greatness to achievements or function, they define character attributes about the nature of God. Therefore, when Greatness is something you achieve, then you are always striving for something you can obtain momentarily but also lose.

When Greatness is who you are, then everything you do has the potential to be great. There is no limit in time to your Greatness and there is no limit to the level of that Greatness. We know that our God is great, we struggle with understanding that we, too, are great.

It is when we truly have an understanding and revelation of our Greatness in God, that Greatness is not something that we are working towards, but something we are drawing from. His Greatness is manifest in and through us, in all things, for the world to see.

This is not just an Old Testament view of God. Jesus so embodied the idea of Greatness that the disciples constantly argued over who was the greatest. Yet Christ didn't chastise them for this line of thinking. He didn't command them to be meek or timid, to have a respectable level of humility. Instead, He showed them what Greatness is. Jesus Christ fostered a sense of Greatness because He himself walked in a revelation of Greatness. It was who He was and He released others to walk in it as well.

Right now God wants to reveal His Greatness in you, not just to you. Greatness is not something that you have to understand; you have to receive. As a Christian, made in the image of God, with Christ in you, you are great. Reflecting anything less than that diminishes the perceived awesomeness of our

God.   Any thought contrary to the idea of your Greatness is a lie that did not originate from the Father. We get to come into full agreement now with the truth of God and who He says we are, in Him.

Take a moment, right now, wherever you are, say, "I am great." Say it out louder, "I am GREAT!" For most people it may feel weird saying that, out loud, about yourself. You don't mind saying your spouse is great or your kids are great, but "I am great?" If people are around you, it might feel even stranger. Many of the truths of God, spoken over ourselves, do sound weird.   The hesitancy to proclaim Greatness over ourselves has been a big victory that the enemy has won in our current Christian culture.

The Bible is full of scriptures about both the power of our tongue and the spoken Word of God.   The tongue has the power of life and death. **Proverbs 18:21 says,** *"Death and life are in the power of the tongue, and those who love it will eat its fruit."*

James 3:4-5 tells us that the tongue can steer us like a rudder steers a ship. It has so much power. Where are you allowing what you speak over yourself to steer you?   What would happen if, instead, you began to speak Greatness over yourself?   What is the worst that could happen? Why is it we are more willing to speak the lies of the enemy, our culture, and of society over us than to speak the truths of what God says about us and what He speaks over us?

Ephesians 4:29 says the only words that come out of our mouths should be words to build up, encourage, and bring life. The words you speak over yourself should be life bringing. What would happen if the words you spoke over the current situations in your life (job, finances, relationships, or family) were life bringing? What current battle you are facing? What if you stopped basing what you proclaim on what you feel or see and come out of agreement with what the enemy wants? Instead, come into agreement with what God has already spoken and said about the situation. In other words, what would happen if you spoke from a place of Greatness, authority, power, and dominion by speaking life?

This is more than a prayer. At least it is more than a prayer as you may understand praying. Culturally, praying has been reduced to asking God for something or thanking Him for something. We do not belittle the power of prayer. But this booklet isn't about prayer. It contains declarations of what God has already spoken. We are declaring His truth over our lives, our homes, our family, and our circumstances. We know the heart of God and are empowering it in our lives as we speak it out with authority.

In Genesis when God spoke, He created. He spoke and things started happening, shifting, transforming. In the New Testament, Jesus spoke to the wind and the waves and they listened and obeyed.   Likewise, when we speak the Word of God in the authority and the Greatness of who we are in Him, we create supernatural possibilities that once were not there. Declaring His Kingdom come, His will be done, begins activation in our lives now.

Declaration proclaims the Word of the Lord on a matter given to us: His children, His family, heirs to the throne, royalty, kings and queens in the Kingdom. It has been established in His court and now we get to establish it on the Earth. We don't just speak it out, we decree it!   Through declaration we shift atmospheres,   move   mountains,   and   speak transformation into any and every situation.

 Moses said, in Deuteronomy 5:5 *"I stood between the Lord and you at that time, to declare to you the Word of the Lord!"* And Job 22:28 says, *"You will also declare a thing, and it will be established for you; and light will shine on your ways!"*

Today is a great day to press into God and get His final and finished Word on love, provision, healing, breakthrough, anointing, outpouring, faith, and hope operating in your life. Declare it and see it done! 1 Chronicles 16:24 says *"Declare His glory among the nations, His wonders among all peoples!"*

In this little booklet are 40 declarations to speak out over yourself and your life. They are declarations that are in line with the Word God has already spoken over you. When you read them, take time to speak them out loud. Hear yourself declare what God has spoken over you. Choose to come out of agreement with the lies of the enemy and what you may have been told. Choose to come into agreement with His Word. Allow yourself to hear His truths, about you and every situation you face.

Romans 10:17 says that faith comes by hearing and hearing by the Word of God. Allow His Word to build a faith within you that can move mountains.

Choose to walk in the Greatness that is in you.

40 days of
DECLARATIONS

HOPE

Day 1

Hope is not a fairytale belief – a whim on which you put your faith. Hope carries the power to align you with the Kingdom of God. Hope is the substance from which faith is birthed and supernatural realities are created. Jeremiah 29:11 says God has a plan and a desire to give us Hope. The Word also tells us the power of the Holy Spirit abounds in Hope. What is faith or belief without Hope?

Hope releases endless God possibilities in our lives

Hope releases endless God possibilities in our lives. It is the ability to tap into the power of Heaven and release potential into today. God tells us to abide in faith, Hope and love. Hope creates a foundation on which belief can be built and faith can be launched. Release a declaration of Hope into your life and live in Greatness. What are you hoping for today?

"May the God of hope fill you with all joy and peace in believing, that by the power of the Holy Spirit you may abound in hope." Romans 15:13

HOPE

Day 1

Today,

I declare **HOPE!**

I will not be discouraged or dissuaded from my passions, my dreams, my promises, and what God has spoken over my life, my family, my home, my region, my workplace, my school, and my destiny. I raise my expectations to super-natural realms and open my eyes to heavenly possibilities.

I am not limited by my own abilities, talents, weaknesses, knowledge, or personal resources. God has me here in this time, for this moment. He has equipped me abundantly for all that He has placed before me. I choose joy, peace, love and faith as I walk that which is before me.

I am excited for today, as today has been charged a day of Greatness!

"For I know the plans I have for you, declares the LORD, plans to prosper you and not to harm you, plans to give you hope and a future."
Jeremiah 29:11

STRENGTH

Day 2

Strength

Psalms 28:7 says that the Lord is our **Strength**. 2 Corinthians 12:9 says that His Strength is made perfect in our weakness. Choosing to trust in His Strength does not negate our responsibilities when facing situations. Ephesians 6:13 tells us when we have done all to stand, stand! The importance of declaring Strength in our lives comes from knowing the source of that Strength.

When Nehemiah 8:10 says that the joy of the Lord is our Strength, it is saying the *fullness* of Him is our Strength. When we are full of God, His Word over our life, His love, His goodness, His purpose, when He is our source, it is from *that place* when we have done all to stand, we can stand!

Today is not just a declaration of His Strength in your life, but the fullness of Him in your life. As you declare Strength today, declare the fullness of God in every area of your life, family, dreams and destiny. You can declare no area of lack of His fullness, so that when you have done all you can do to stand, you stand firm and strong. Stand in the knowledge of who your Christ is, what He has done, and what He has promised to do!

STRENGTH

Day 2

Today,

I declare **STRENGTH!**

I will not be weary or weak. I will passionately and personally pursue divine encounters today with my Creator, my Father, and the lover of my soul. I will run with the direct attempt to win; in my running there will be no weariness. I break off any fatigue, exhaustion, tiredness, and lack of focus. I declare strength to my legs to stand in the midst of my calling, my destiny.

I speak supernatural joy over my life, my family, my work place, my school and my region, which gives me heavenly Strength. I gladly face the challenges of today and walk in the knowledge that the victory is already won.

I declare that today will be a great day because I am prepared for Greatness!

"He gives strength to the weary and increases the power of the weak." Isaiah 40:29

Strength in our lives comes from knowing the source of that Strength

VISION

Day 3

Vision

The Declaration of **Vision** is not just about the ability to see what is there. Rather, it is the ability to prophetically see what is not there. "God, open our eyes to the supernatural potentials of what we can do and accomplish through and in You." Sometimes it is so easy to see the giants in the land, but not see the promise.

The promise is what God is longing to do. It is the Word over our life, our marriage, our family, our job, our workplace, and over our dreams. We are declaring to our supernatural eyes the ability to have heavenly focus, raised expectations, and divine potential.

God is always at work, in every situation and circumstance. We get to chose to come into agreement with what He is already doing and declare that we will no longer be hindered by the lack of what we are seeing in the physical. We are declaring He will show us purpose and release Vision to us in every circumstance and that our steps will be ordered by Him.

So today we declare VISION!

Day 3

Today,

I declare **VISION!**

I will not be limited by what I physically see or have seen. I speak over my eyes that they will be opened to supernatural promises. I declare the redemptive revelation of God over my dreams, my calling, my family, my home, my neighborhood, my city, my church, and my region. I see with eyes of possibility. I see with eyes of hope. I see with eyes of love.

I break off all distractions and discouragements. I declare heavenly focus as I press on towards the high calling on my life.

Today will be a great day, for today I will see Greatness!

"Then the Lord answered me and said, write the vision, and make it plain on tablets, that he may run who reads it!" Habakkuk 2:2

Vision (Webster's Definition)
- The ability to see: sight or eyesight
- Something you imagine
- Something you see or dream

Day 4

More

When we declare "**More**" in our lives, we release the supernatural abundance of Heaven. God does not just want to meet our needs, He wants to exceed our expectations. He is the God of abundance and overflow. David says in the Psalms that "His cup runs over." Our declaration is not just that God meet us in our current difficulty or circumstance, but that God moves through us to affect everyone around us. I don't want to be just blessed; I want to be a blessing.

In the book of Matthew it says blessed are those who hunger and thirst for they shall be filled. That is not about having a beggar's mentality. Our Father is a good Father giving good gifts, who is not raising a community of beggars and paupers. This is not about need, this is about want. God meets needs, but he exceeds desires.

As sons and daughters we can break off a poverty mindset that lives within natural limitations and begin to declare the abundance of Heaven in our lives, marriage, relationships, jobs, and our dreams. It is time to start living in the More!

"Blessed are those hunger and thirst for righteousness, for they shall be filled." Matthew 5:6

Day 4

Today,

I declare **MORE!**

I stir hunger, desire and the pursuit of all the promises of Heaven manifested in my life. I break off complacency, laziness and the lies of the enemy that say this is all there is. Today, I place a demand on the Heavens that must be met. I release supernatural abundance into my home, my work-place, my school, my city, **and my family. I enlarge my dreams and my vision to heavenly realms.**

I break off any lie of lack and release the kingly **promise of More. Today, I don't just declare Greatness,** I live Greatness!

Blessed are those who hunger and thirst for they shall be filled!

"And Jabez called on the God of Israel saying, 'Oh, that You would bless me indeed, and enlarge my territory, that Your hand would be with me, and that You would keep me from evil, that I may not cause pain.' So God granted him what he requested."
1 Chronicles 4:10

GREATNESS

Day 5

Greatness

The Declaration of **Greatness** is not about us or about our ability. Scripture says that our God is a Great God, and that God resides in each and every one of us. Therefore, His Greatness should be present and obvious in our lives. The declaration of His Greatness is a declaration of His total rule and authority in every situation and circumstance in our lives.

As we declare His Greatness in relationships, over our health, our job, over our school, or community, we are declaring His preeminence. We are placing Him as the head and rule; and we are making a statement of faith that activates the supernatural and places things in heavenly order. It is truly His kingdom being established on this earth, in our lives and in our communities. That call of Greatness has less to do with us, and everything to do with Him - which in return has everything to do with us!

Greatness living is mandatory living for every Christian who declares they have Christ living in them.

Today will be a great day
because **I DECLARE GREATNESS**

GREATNESS

Day 5

Today,

I declare **GREATNESS!**

I will not be limited by my talents or my abilities. I will not be defined by my weaknesses. I have been equipped with resources in heavenly realms and have been given all authority. Today, I cast off worries. Today, I cast off fears. Today, I walk in boldness and confidence that the good work God has started in me, in my family, in my job, in my school, He will complete, in me and through me.

Today, I break off false humility that may keep me from laying hold of my destiny. I break off any pride that may push me away from my destiny. Today, I am choosing to seek out and find the great in all situations and circumstances. I break off the lies of defeat and I have a renewed mind of Greatness.

Today will be a great day because I declare Greatness!

"I will proclaim your greatness, my God and King; I will thank you forever and ever!" Psalm 145:1

JOY

Day 6

Joy

When we declare **Joy** over our lives we are making a conscious choice to choose joy despite our circumstances. Joy is not a result of our circumstances, but a declaration to our circumstances. James 1 tells us to count it all joy. That is our choice, our decision. In choosing Joy we release Joy. By counting any circumstance all Joy we release the fullness of God into that circumstance and into our life. When we count our marriage all Joy, we release the fullness of God into our marriage. When we decide to count our work all Joy, we release the fullness of God in our workplace.

Where the fullness of God resides, anything that is not of Him must be transformed into His image, or must go. What is His image? God's image is love! So deciding to declare joy and choosing it today ultimately releases supernatural love into our lives and every circumstance. It is the Joy of the Lord, His fullness, and ultimately His love, that is our strength!

Today is a great day to choose Joy, declare Joy, and a great day to LIVE IT!

"But the harvest of the Spirit is love, joy, peace patience, kindness, goodness, fidelity, gentleness and self control." Galatians 5:22

Day 6

Today,

I declare JOY!

I release the supernatural dispensation of Joy upon me, my family and my destiny! I break off discouragement, doubt, and bind the spirit of **depression. I decide today to count it Joy in all things I** place my hand to: my work, my passions, and my responsibilities.

I speak a renewing over my mind and my attitude and a refreshing in my spirit. I tap into the unlimited resources of Heaven that have equipped me for this day, this moment, this journey.

I am excited and joyful about what lays before me, for I have been chosen for such a time as this!

"...Do not sorrow, for the JOY of the Lord is your strength!" Nehemiah 8:10

Joy is a declaration to our circumstances

ADVANCE

Day 7

Advance

The Declaration to **Advance** is a powerful declaration and statement on many levels. First, we are choosing and stating publicly that we are moving from the old and stepping into the new – no matter the cost, risk, or battle we may face. We are choosing to leave behind old habits, old ways of thinking, old (and perhaps harmful) lifestyles. We are embracing the promises of what God has in store for us.

The declaration to Advance proclaims to the land (and to the promise) that we are moving forward, laying claim, and grabbing hold of what has been promised. It serves as notice to anything currently inhabiting the land of our destiny that we are moving forward. We will walk in the calling, the dream, and the vision of what is rightfully ours.

The declaration to Advance allows those we are journeying with to hold us accountable, encourage us, and challenge us not to turn back, look back or go back: to old habits, lifestyles, or old ways of thinking.

Before we can Advance, we must first choose to Advance. It is in that choice and that declaration that advancing becomes possible.

Day 7

Today,

I declare I will **ADVANCE!**

I will not back down. I will not retreat. I am moving forward. I am laying hold of my destiny, walking in the promises of God for me, and I am taking land. I am leaving behind old habits, old addictions, (old mindsets), and old bondage and am walking in the new.

I am a new creation with a renewed mind and fresh vision. I am walking in my dreams, my visions, and the promises over my life. Today, I will pursue a fresh encounter with God, a personal relationship with Christ, and a powerful outpouring of the Holy Spirit.

Today, I declare is a day of Greatness because I am moving in Greatness!

"See the Lord your God has given you the land, go up and take possession of it!" Deuteronomy 1:21

Today I will pursue a fresh encounter with **God**

Day 8

New

With the Declaration of **New**, we release the redemptive power of God into our lives, circumstances, and every situation we face today. New isn't just a fresh start; but, rather, a redeemed start. Many times we are looking for God to release us from a situation, relationship, or circumstance. Yet God has often placed or positioned us in such a way that we may be a blessing in the situation.

Isaiah says that God brings springs in the desert and roads in the wilderness. He makes all things New. God wants to make your circumstance New today by transforming it; creating a way were there seems to be no way. He wants to be the breakthrough in your wilderness right now by working in you and through you.

The power of experiencing His New usually requires a shift in our perspective.

*"I shall open the rivers in desolate heights,
and fountains in the midst of the valleys; I will make
the wilderness a pool of water, and the dry land
springs of water."* Isaiah 41:18

Day 8

Today,

I declare **NEW**!

I declare New life, New opportunities, New hope, New love, and New favor over me, my family, my home, my work, my dreams, and my destiny. I open my eyes and raise my expectations to see New vision. I renew my mind and allow the praise of the Lord to be on my lips or on my tongue.

Today, I will declare the goodness of a good God in every area of my life. I break off old habits, old mindsets, old and tired functions as I walk in the New and fresh anointing of God! I speak His mercies over me, His goodness over me, His grace over me, His strength over me today!

I declare today will be a great day because today is a New day!

"Behold I am doing a new thing, Now it springs forth..."
Isaiah 43:19

"The steadfast love of the Lord never ceases; His mercies never come to an end; they are new every morning; great is your faithfulness!" Lamentations 3:22-23

WHOLENESS

Day 9

Wholeness

The Declaration of **Wholeness** is the power to release the finished work of the cross into our lives. Not only did God, through Jesus, release the full power of healing for our lives physically, but He heals emotional wounds and relational scars as well.

God desires for us to be complete, lacking nothing. First He heals, then He restores. Where we have lost joy or peace, where we have lost faith or hope, God longs to restore. David prays in the Psalms that God would restore his joy. We get to pray and declare restoration in our lives as well.

We are shifting our focus from our circumstance, our lack, and our hurt, to declaring His Wholeness, His restoration, His healing in our lives and in our circumstance.

"Restore to me the joy of salvation and uphold me by Your generous spirit." Psalm 51:12

God desires us to be **COMPLETE**

WHOLENESS

Day 9

Today,

I declare WHOLENESS!

I speak the peace of God over my mind and body. I speak perfect health over every cell and system in my body. I take authority over any disease, illness, or malady affecting my body and command all things that do not line up to God's design and kingdom to go in the name of Jesus! I speak the finished work of the Cross over my spirit, soul and body. I am Whole, healed from all wounds, disappointments and abuses from the past. I break off all wrong thinking, victim thinking, and speak victory over the battle of my mind. I break off loneliness, depression, and isolation.

Today, I declare supernatural health over myself, my home, my work place, and my school. I am equipped today to fulfill all that I am called to be.

Today, I will live in Greatness because I have been called great!

"Now may the God of peace make you holy in every way, and may your whole spirit and soul and body be kept blameless until our Lord Jesus Christ comes again. God will make this happen, for He who calls you is faithful." 1 Thessalonians 5:23-24

RESTORATION

Day 10

Restoration

When we declare **Restoration** in our lives, we release the redeeming power of God. His redemptive power can Restore relationships, dreams, and friendships, and it can mend hearts. The Restoration of God is far reaching; not limited by time or our circumstances. It is greater than our fears, our regrets, and more comprehensive than what we can do in our own strength.

In Psalm 23 David calls God the Shepherd who restores his soul. Joel 2 says God can restore the things and time that the enemy has stolen. What are you asking God to Restore in your life: Hope? Joy? Peace? Love? His timing is perfect, His methods infallible. Rather than just look at your lack, declare to your lack the fullness of the power and provision of your God.

God will shift your circumstances to create breakthrough, springs in the desert, and a way in the wilderness.

"The One who sat on the throne said, 'I am making all things new.'" Revelation 21:5

"For I will restore health to you and your wounds will heal." Jeremiah 30:17

RESTORATION

Day 10

Today,

I declare **RESTORATION!**

Nothing has been lost in the Kingdom. I release restoration in my family, my home, my job, and all of my relationships. I speak renewed life into my dreams and visions. I lay hold of the prophetic destiny over my life and my family. I declare kingdom restoration into my finances and into my health. I release the Kairos* time of Heaven.

I know that the Word of the Lord is true and unfailing and that what He has said, will be. I stand on His promises and His faithfulness and so I release renewed hope and faith into my life and a fresh outlook into my day!

Today will be a great day because nothing is lost in the Kingdom. Today I will walk in Greatness!

"Restore unto me the joy of your salvation and renew a right spirit within me." Psalm 51:12

*Kairos: appointed time; opportune moment; suitable or appropriate time for something to occur or be accomplished.

REVIVAL

Day 11

Revival

When we declare **Revival** we have to shift our perspective. Our ability to truly grasp and understand this will help us establish His kingdom in our lives. We are not simply praying for Revival for others. It is God's heart to see the lost saved and the broken hearted restored and come to Him. Yet, it is important to first declare Revival in our own lives. This is a declaration that the lifeless areas of our lives would be revived in Him. Where there is hardness of heart or walls of hurt and distrust that we have built, we invite God to come into our lives, begin to breathe life, and break down those walls.

When Elijah prayed to God a fire came and consumed the sacrifice. We are the sacrifice of praise to God. We are saying Lord, come and consume me, ignite a passion within me, fuel a desire for more of you and to meet with you. It is in that place where revival is birthed and it is in that place where we come alive.

Today, **GREATNESS** starts with me

REVIVAL

Day 11

Today,

I declare **REVIVAL!**

I release the supernatural power of a mighty God into my heart, my home, my church, my work, my school, my region! I move in a spirit of repentance and brokenness as I press into God's word over me and my destiny.

I raise my expectations to see great signs and wonders, miracles, and breakthrough in my life and the lives of those around me today. I will not settle and I will not be satisfied with anything less than the **fullness of the promises of God manifest around me.**

I call on the former and the latter rain of the Holy Spirit to pour out all across this land and move on hearts in power, bringing them an encounter with an awesome God!

Today, Greatness starts with me and I will bring Greatness everywhere I go!

"Will you not revive us again, that your people may rejoice in you?" Psalm 85:6

Day 12

Peace

The declaration of **Peace** is not the absence of agitation or struggles. Declaring Peace does not mean we expect everything to stop and we just sit down in a nice comfy chair to take a nap for fifteen minutes. Peace is not the absence of war; it is the presence of His righteousness manifested in our lives and in every situation. It is an invitation for the presence of God and His righteousness to be revealed in our circumstances.

The Word says that His Peace surpasses understanding. This means the understanding in a circumstance or moment may not be peaceable. However, when we give it to God and release His presence and His righteousness into the situation, we are able to rise above understanding and be a supernaturally redeemed people who walk in authority and power.

Today, allow the Peace of God to permeate in and through your life.

PEACE

Day 12

Today,

I declare **PEACE!**

I release the supernatural and divine nature of God into my home, my school, my workplace, and into all areas of my life. I break off confusion, doubt, and fear from my life, my dreams, my destiny, and my circumstances. I press deep into the arms of Christ and allow Him to direct my path.

Today I will be great because God made today great

I refresh in the renewing waters of Holy Spirit as He moves through me. I renew my mind and vision and walk in the understanding that all things are possible. I declare a war of Peace over any area of my life not in line with the Kingdom of God!

Today will be great because God made today great!

"Peace I leave with you; my peace I give to you. Not as the world gives do I give to you. Let not your hearts be troubled, neither let them be afraid."
John 14:27

REFRESHING

Day 13

Refreshing

The **Refreshing** of the Lord can renew even the most weary and can restore areas of our lives that feel burned out and dry. Every piece of machinery needs both water to keep it from overheating and oil to keep it functioning without burning out. Just as in our lives, while pursuing our dreams and desires or just functioning in daily life, we must stay both refreshed in the cooling waters of the Lord (His wellsprings), and filled with the oil of the Holy Ghost.

Even when you do not see a way, God's Word says He makes a way in the wilderness and streams in the wasteland. Today, declare the Refreshing of God in your life and your circumstances. Choose to see Him create a way where you do not see a way; hope where you have seen only hopelessness. He is a good God who refreshes and it is in Him we are renewed.

"I will refresh the weary and satisfy the faint."
Jeremiah 31:25

Day 13

Today,

I declare **REFRESHING!**

I will not grow weary and I will not grow faint as I press into my destiny, dreams and calling for my life and my family. I release into my life the refreshing waters of the Holy Spirit to restore and renew.

I break off old habits, old mindsets, old addictions, old ways, and I speak that today all things are new! I speak strength into weakness, hope into weariness, faith into discouragement, and I walk in love, joy and peace today!

Today will be great because today I am taking Greatness with me everywhere I go!

"He refreshes my soul. He guides me along right paths for His name's sake." Psalms 23:3

I release into my life the refreshing waters of the **Holy Spirit**

RIGHTEOUSNESS

Day 14

Righteousness

Declaring the **Righteousness** of God brings things into alignment, into Rightness with who God is, His will, and His kingdom. When we declare the Righteousness of God, we speak into the chaos of · a situation, relationship, or feeling, and call it into the rightness with the one true King. We call things out of order to come into order with His kingdom and the divine order of Heaven.

Today, as you speak the Righteousness of God into your life, relationships, and situations, release them into His divine will and order. Allow His Kingdom to truly come into your circumstances and be established in your life.

"The Prayer of the righteous man avails much!"
James 5:16

Righteousness of God brings things into alignment

RIGHTEOUSNESS

Day 14

Today,

I declare **RIGHTEOUSNESS!**

I release the righteous judgments of Heaven into every situation of my life. Today, I walk in health, provision, protection and relationship with the Father. My steps have been ordered, my path is set, and my focus is renewed. No weapon against me shall prosper, no word against me shall rule.

I walk under the covering of Heaven and the Word of God that says I have been hand picked for such a time as this, that I am chosen, I am royalty; and, in Christ, I have overcome!

Today will be great because I have laid hold of Greatness!

*"For the eyes of the Lord are on the righteous
and His ears are attentive to their prayer!"*
1 Peter 3:12

LOVE

Day 15

Love of God

The **Love** of God is so much more than just a feel-good sensation or experience. When we allow the Love of God to permeate our lives, it gives Him access to the heart of who we are. His heart speaks into our heart, the core of us. God's words, His truth, and life-transforming promises spoken into us, through us, and over us, and take us from glory to glory. Love isn't just something that God does, it is who He is!

Everything God does, every word He speaks, every promise He makes comes from a place of love. His is an unconditional, right where you are, just as you are, kind of Love. To truly access that Love and experience that Love, we have to allow ourselves to be vulnerable and transparent about who we are to God.

We have to be raw and real with the revelation of who He is to us and how He sees us, so that truth can supersede all else. It is there that Love moves beyond being a concept and into a true reality.

> Everything **God** does every word He speaks, every promise He makes comes from a place of **LOVE**

LOVE

Day 15

Today,

I declare LOVE!

I release the overwhelming and supernatural love of God in my life. I allow myself to be saturated and intoxicated in its goodness. I break off all fear, doubt, and anxiety over my dreams, passions and destiny, and I walk in the fullness of the Love of the Father. I restore my identity as a child of the King, royalty, and chosen.

Today, I allow love to move in me, through me, and saturate all that is around me. I choose to love my family, my neighbors, my coworkers, and to press into the love of my Heavenly Father. In His Love there are no restrictions. In His Love, there are no limitations. In His Love there is no end!

Today will be a great day because today I will LOVE greatly!

"For I am convinced that neither death nor life, neither angels nor demons neither the present nor the future, nor any powers, neither height nor depth, nor anything else in all of creation will be able to separate us from the love of God that is in Christ Jesus our Lord!" Romans 8:38-39

-45

Day 16

Life

God is the giver of **Life**. There is a difference between simply living and being alive. I love the quote from the movie *Braveheart*, "All men die but not all men truly live." As Christians we are supposed to be those who truly live and live abundantly. That is the heart of God toward us, abundant Life. Many times we do not want Life more abundantly because we are struggling with the life we have right now. Therefore, we must make the distinction between functional living and abundant living.

The life God wants to give us is not about more errands, busyness, or rushing the kids from point A to point B. Nor does He want us to face more trails, battles, frustrations, and hurts. The Life He gives is a Life that is filled with joy unspeakable, peace beyond understanding, grace, mercy, and patience.

That is the DNA of Heaven, the very essence of our God. It is His love moving in and through us that gives us Life.

"...I have come that they may have life, and that they may have it more abundantly." John 10:10

Day 16

Today,

I declare LIFE!

I release the abundance of Heaven and the overflow of God's refreshing and encouragement into me today. I speak goodness and mercy into my home, my work, my school, my dreams, and my destiny. I break off any lie or attack of the enemy that would try to diminish, restrict or kill the abundant life in me.

Today, I will walk in the way of the Lord; I will saturate in His truths, and I will experience the wholeness of His life. Today, I release life into my vision and raise my expectations. I release life into my outlook and see possibilities. I release life into my relationships and receive encouragement and friendship. I release life into my speech and speak life into others.

Today will be a great day because I am ALIVE to live greatly!

The thief comes only to steal and to kill and to destroy. I have come that they may have life, and that they have it more **abundantly** John 10:10

WONDERS

Day 17

Wonders

We have a God of **Wonders**. Psalm 40:5 says, "*O LORD my God, you have performed many wonders for us. Your plans for us are too numerous to list.*" So many times we limit our ability to receive God's miracles by trying to figure out our own solutions instead. Of course, we want God to help us with our plan for our life or situation. We have a God who is so much greater than us; His ways are not our ways, His solutions are not always our solutions.

Instead of trying to figure out how to fix everything in our lives, we need to begin to declare the Wonders of God of in our lives. We need to allow ourselves to be amazed at His goodness and faithfulness and fall in love with a God who is great and mighty. Psalm 136 says we should give thanks to the Lord for He alone does great wonders.

God is not just a God of Wonders, He has so many wonders that He is wonder-*full*!

"Oh give thanks to the Lord of lords for His mercy endures forever: to Him who alone does great wonders. His mercy endures forever."
Psalm 136:3-4

Day 17

Today,

I declare **WONDERS!**

I release heavenly solutions and kingdom revelations to invade my life, my family, my work, my dreams, and my destiny. My eyes will be opened to see supernatural possibilities walls will be torn down and mountains moved on my behalf.

I stir up my faith, I raise my expectations, and I walk in the fullness of my God. I give no place to doubt, I silence the lies of fear, and I shun evil. I release creative miracles, heavenly provision, and kingdom protection over all to which I place my hand.

Today, I will see Greatness because everything I touch will be great!

"Praise the Lord, for He has shown me the Wonders of His unfailing Love." Psalm 31:21

We have a God of **Wonders**

LAUGHTER

Day 18

Laughter

It is said that **Laughter** is the result of the irony of a situation. Many of the situations that we face are ironic because what the enemy has intended for harm God will use as a blessing in our life. Laughter need not be simply based on feelings; it can be based on the knowledge of the promises of God and the release of the Holy Spirit in our lives and our circumstances.

When we allow the joy of the Lord to bubble up in our lives, it begins to spill out into the lives of those around us as well. Laughter can become an uncontainable, unstoppable force of the goodness of God that spreads like wildfire, establishing Christ's Kingdom.

Today, despite what you are facing or going through, declare Laughter in your life.

"Blessed are you who weep now, for you shall laugh."
Luke 6:21

Laughter can become an
uncontainable, unstoppable force

LAUGHTER

Day 18

Today,

I declare **LAUGHTER!**

I release an abundance of the joy of the Lord in my life, my work, my family, my home, my dreams, and my visions. Let it fill me up, let it rise up within me, and let it overflow through me. I release the uncontainable, limitless and abounding goodness of God in and through my life. Let love move me, joy overwhelm me, and laughter spring from my heart! Let laughter say to the enemy, "You have no power, you have no authority, and my God reigns!"

I will not be moved or swayed by my circumstances; I stand firm on my God's promises. I allow His Spirit to fill me and rivers of living water to abound in me.

Today Greatness is found in the abundance of His joy as it comes out of me!

"The Lord laughs at the wicked..." Psalm 37:13

"He will fill your mouth with laughter and your lips with shouting." Job 8:21

FORGIVENESS

Day 19

Forgiveness

Our ability to choose **Forgiveness** is the gateway for much healing in our lives. You can be doing everything 100% correctly; but when you hold on to unforgiveness, it keeps you bound and holds you back from moving forward. Forgiveness softens our hardened hearts and opens us up to healing and wholeness. It softens us to the voice of God and the yearnings of the Holy Spirit in us.

Forgiveness is a key to our ability to encounter the **Father's embrace. So often we think that forgiveness** is just saying sorry, or telling someone that you forgive them for what they have done. Forgiveness is also about being willing to let go of the hurt, the pain. True Forgiveness lets go of the offense and holds on to the truth of God, which is His word over our lives and our circumstance.

Today, choose to Forgive and walk in freedom and the fullness of God.

"For if you forgive men their trespasses, your Heavenly Father will also forgive you. But if you do not forgive men their trespasses, neither will your Father forgive your trespasses." Matthew 6:14-15

FORGIVENESS

Day 19

Today,

I Declare **FORGIVENESS!**

I release the overwhelming love of a good God into all areas of my life and I choose to let go of offense, hurt, bitterness, and anger. I release and set free those who have offended and hurt me. I place them and the circumstances into the hands of a good and mighty **God.** I set myself free of all resentment and restore my value established as a child of the Most High. I allow healing to flood my heart, this situation, my home, my work, my destiny and my dreams. **It is time to press forward and no longer be hindered by the past.**

Today, I replace the hurt and the pain of the situation with the Forgiveness and gladness of the Spirit. I will walk in both the fullness of Forgiveness and the Father's love. Today will be a great day because I have allowed Greatness to flood my life.

"He who covers and forgives and offense seeks love..." Proverbs 17:9

"Be gentle and forbearing with one another and, if one has a difference (A grievance or complaint) against another, readily pardoning each other; even as the Lord has freely forgiven you so must you do also!" Colossians 3:13

GROWTH

Day 20

Growth

A declaration of **Growth** speaks to any area where we are stalled, halted, or are hindered. As a Christian we are to go from glory to glory. That includes growth, increase, development in our maturity and relationship with the Father, our walk in the Lord, and our ability to showcase His Kingdom.

Growth looks different in each life. Sometimes Growth is internal, a slow process of healing and maturing. Sometimes it is external with advancement and expansion in our lives.

When we declare the Growth of the Lord, we are speaking the fullness of His promises over our lives and each area where we are hindered. We are not just speaking life, but life abundantly and overflowing.

"...only God Who makes it grow and become greater!" 1 Corinthians 3:7

I allow myself to be planted in the rich soil of **Kingdom**

GROWTH

Day 20

Today,

I declare **GROWTH**!

I speak to the areas that are stalled or stunted and I speak kingdom life! I release areas of immaturity, stubbornness, and irresponsibility. I allow the Spirit of God to fill me and manifest spiritual maturity needed to sustain heavenly destinies.

I allow myself to be planted in the rich soil of Kingdom community, that I may experience spiritual growth that will allow me to affect my work, my home, my school, my region, my family and my dreams.

I allow the perfecting waters of the Holy Spirit to pour over me, saturate me, refresh me, transform me, and allow me to grow into the child of God I am supposed to be.

Today ,I am growing in Greatness, therefore the fruit of my life will be GREAT!

"Planted in the house of the Lord, they shall flourish in the courts of our God!" Psalm 92:13

FAVOR

Day 21

Favor

As a Christian we are highly **Favored**. We are partnered with the Creator of the universe, the King of Kings, and the Most High God. We were not designed to trudge through this life barely making it and scraping by. We are created to be more than conquerors, we are overcomers. We are filled with the Holy Spirit and equipped with every spiritual blessing, so we can be living that way.

Matthew 17:20 says we walk with divine wisdom and knowledge, move in power, and can speak to mountains and they will be cast into the sea. A declaration of Favor is to align us with the will of God and what He is doing in our lives, circumstances, circles of influence and region.

Today, allow His Spirit and Favor to flow through you.

"...I say to you, if you have faith as a mustard seed, you will say to this mountain, 'Move from here to there,' and it will move and nothing will be impossible for you." Matthew 17:20

FAVOR

Day 21

Today,

I declare **FAVOR**!

I speak to closed doors that they will open, and to obstacles that they will be removed. I speak supernatural resources and the abundance of Heaven regarding jobs, better jobs, pay raises, and found monies. Friendships will be strengthened and restored, relationships will be renewed and refreshed, and my dreams will be enlarged.

Today, my steps are ordered by God. Today, I will walk in the fullness of destiny. I declare heavenly opportunities, supernatural meetings, righteous judgments, and the Kingdom manifested in my life.

Today, I will take hold of Greatness and see that everywhere I go is great!

"I will look on you with favor and make you fruitful and increase your numbers, and I will keep my covenant with you!" Leviticus 26:9

"For whoever finds me finds life and receives favor from the Lord!" Proverbs 8:35

POWER

Day 22

Power

The book of Acts tells us that we receive **Power** when the Holy Spirit comes upon us. The declaration of Power is about coming into agreement with what God has already released. It is important to receive that Power so that it can be manifested in our lives. It is a Power that is beyond feelings or circumstances, greater than opinions and understanding. This Power is not of this world, but of God's Kingdom and says, "I can do all things in and through Christ."

Knowing about the Power, having an understanding that there is Power, and what the Power is capable of doing, is very different from receiving the power, and living in the power. Power must be greater than the knowledge of its existence; it is the ability to receive it, come into agreement with it, and walk in it.

Today, as you declare His Power in your life, receive it, walk in it, and allow the world to experience the love of a good God through you.

> ## I can do all things in and through **Christ**

POWER

Day 22

Today,

I declare **POWER!**

I speak supernatural and abundant strength into my life. I release a heavenly outpouring of the glory of God into my family, workplace, school, dreams, and destiny. I will not be limited by my own strength or ability because I am resourced with all of Heaven and I am enabled by the Holy Spirit for Greater works today.

Today, nothing can stop, hinder, diminish or lessen the full force of the Spirit of God working in and through me. I open my eyes to see the miraculous, I lift my faith to be a force of healing, I renew hope to bring life, and I release Power into everything to which I lay my hand.

Today, Greatness will be seen in the power of a Great God!

"I pray...that out of His glorious riches He may strengthen you with Power through His Spirit in your inner being." Ephesians 3:16

Day 23

Awe

I remember singing a song in my youth group to God, "I stand. I stand in **Awe** of you." I had to ask, "What does Awe mean?" My youth pastor replied that Awe is when you are so amazed by the goodness of God you do not even have the words to describe it.

The declaration of Awe in our lives releases a wave of God's goodness so great that we have no words to describe it. It allows God's goodness, His favor, His love, His peace to rush in and overwhelm us and every adverse circumstance we face.

In the midst of the chaos and the hectic business of life it is easy to loose site of the grandeur of our God and how He is blessing us and moving in and through us. It is easy to get caught up in need and miss the blessings. The Awe of God places us in the proper perspective to be able to realize how amazing He truly is, and how blessed we really are.

We do not just serve a Great God, we serve an *Awe*-some God.

> ## **Awe** releases a wave of God's goodness

Day 23

Today,

I declare AWE!

I am blown away and blessed by the glory and Greatness of my God! I stand in wonder and Awe at His beauty and majesty. I am infused by His mercy and grace. I place a demand on the outrageous outpouring of the Holy Spirit in my life, my home, my work, my school, my dreams and this destiny I am walking in. I release heavenly expectations into my relationships and friendships.

Today, I will be amazed at the goodness of my God. I will walk in Awe at his Awesomeness. I declare that nothing can compare to the Greatness of my God, so today will be a Great Day!

"God is powerful and all must stand in Awe of Him."
Job 25:1

"For the Lord most High is AWESOME and He is a great King over all the earth." Psalm 47:2

REDEMPTION

Day 24

Redemption

When Christ **Redeemed** us, He took everything the enemy tried to use, abuse, and discard, and gave purpose and value to it. Webster's Dictionary defines Redemption as, "to make more capable." When we declare the redemptive power of Christ in our lives, we allow Him to restore areas that seem incapable, useless, worthless, or abandoned. Areas that we felt had no purpose in our lives, God can restore for His glory and to establish His kingdom.

There may be areas of our heart that have become hardened or dreams that we have abandoned. Christ's redemptive power can restore that which is lost, redeem it, give it a purpose, and a hope.

"But as for you, you meant evil against me; but God meant it for good, in order to bring it about as it is this day, to save many people alive."
Genesis 50:20

When Christ **REDEEMED** us, He took everything the enemy tried to use, abuse, and discard, and gave purpose and value to it

REDEMPTION

Day 24

Today,

I declare **REDEMPTION!**

I release the supernatural, outrageous love of a good God in my life, home, work, school, dreams, and destiny! I embrace Gods faithfulness, goodness and righteousness. I Redeem any dream that the enemy has tried to steal, kill, and destroy. I Redeem all good relationships, friendships, and resources. Nothing is lost in the kingdom of a good God. I Redeem all creativity, ideas, and thoughts.

Today, I choose to press into a God that makes all things new. Today, I choose to love on a God that chose me.

Today will be an amazing day of Greatness because my God has made all things great!

"In Him we have redemption through His blood, the forgiveness of sins, according to the riches of His grace." Ephesians 1:7

HEALING

Day 25

Healing

Isaiah 53:5 says that *"...by His stripes we are healed."* Healing was something that was done on the cross at Calvary. It was accomplished through Christ and His sacrifice. When we declare Healing in our bodies we are releasing the promise of God that has already been given to us. We come into alignment with what He has spoken and done.

Healing is not something for which we have to ask God's will. We know we have a God who heals and has healed. We get to come into agreement with what He has already done.

When you declare Healing today you are truly speaking, "Your Kingdom come."

"The Spirit of the Lord is upon me, because He has anointed me to preach the good news to the poor; He has sent me to heal the broken hearted; to proclaim liberty to the captives and recovery of sight to the blind, and to set free all who are oppressed!"

Luke 4:18

HEALING

Day 25

Today,

I declare **HEALING!**

I release the divine manifestation of Heaven into every area of sickness, illness, and any broken area of my life, home, work, and school. I lay hold of my right as a child of the risen King for Healing and restoration in my body, my relationships, and my friendships. I break off every attack of the enemy to hurt me, afflict me, or slow me down, and I come out of agreement with every lie.

I increase my expectations and raise my faith to see supernatural signs, wonders, and Healings in the lives of those around me. I will be a vessel of the goodness of God and I will manifest that goodness to all those I come in contact with.

Today, I will look for opportunities to release Healing to those **who are hurting. My words will bring comfort,** restoration, and wholeness.

Today will be a great day because today I am sharing Greatness with the world!

"Who forgives all your sins, Who heals all of your diseases." Psalm 103:3

WAR

Day 26

War

There are those who say that what will be, will be. That the divine will of God will happen, no matter what. Then there are those who hear the word of Nehemiah 4:14 and say, "Today is a day that I will fight for what is important." Matthew 11:12 says that the Kingdom of God suffers violence and the violent take it by force. A declaration of **War** is one that says, "I will not stay silent any more. I will contend for my family, my city, my region, and the promises of God!"

It is a declaration, not so much about a physical action, but a spiritual one. We call down the promises of God and release heavenly hosts to battle on our behalf and on behalf of the Word of the Lord.

Today, as you make a declaration of War, contend for what God has spoken to you. Lay hold of His promises and refuse to let go.

> **War** contends for promises
> and refuses to let go

Day 26

Today,

I declare I am going to **WAR!**

I lay hold of the promises over myself, my family, my home, work, school, dreams, and destiny. I contend for the fullness of these promises in my life. I break off any and all attacks of the enemy and I come out of agreement with the lies of the devil. I have been **given all** authority in Heaven and on Earth. I have been called and chosen for such a time as this!

The victory has already been assured and the battle won. I am here to enact the justice of God. I come equipped and clothed in the righteous armor of God and wield the active power of the spoken Word. I raise my faith in defiance of the enemy and I War victoriously over powers, principalities, and the ruler of darkness. I tear down every stronghold in my life, my family, my city, and I bind the strong man. In Christ I overcome. In Christ I have victory. In Christ I can do all things.

I declare today will be a great day because I have laid hold of Greatness and I will not let go!

"Do not be afraid Of them. Remember the Lord, great and awesome and fight for your brethren, your sons, your daughters, your wives and homes." Nehemiah 4:14

VICTORY

Day 27

Victory

Today we get to declare **Victory**! A very common saying when I was growing up was, "When the devil reminds you of your past, remind him of his future." Well, better than reminding the enemy of his future, how about reminding you of your future? If we truly believe the Word of God, then we are victorious, in Him, in all things. We are victorious in our health because He is our healer. We are victorious in our finances because He is our provider. We are victorious in our relationships because He is our redeemer and reconciler.

One of the best things we can do today, despite what we are facing right now, is to remind ourselves of how the story ends. We win! We win because Christ won.

Today, as you declare Victory in your life, remind yourself of His promises and the certainty of what Christ has done and won. Walk in the fullness of Victory.

"But thanks be to God, which gives us the Victory through our Lord Jesus Christ!" 1 Corinthians 15:57

VICTORY

Day 27

Today,

I declare **VICTORY!**

I have overcome; I am more than a conqueror and in Christ I have the **Victory**. I am not limited by my ability, hindered by my resources, or restricted by my talents. I declare to every attack or assault on me, my family, my dreams, and my destiny, "You have already failed. You have no power or authority over my life and I break off these attacks in Jesus' name."

I speak to every mountain in my way, "Be moved and cast into the sea!" Today, there will be healing in my body, breakthrough in my work, and restoration in my relationships. Today will be a day of Victory for I am living victoriously! I will not stop. I will not back down. I will not give in. The battle has been won, the ending has been declared, and I am walking in triumph.

Today Greatness is already mine, so I am walking in Greatness!

BREAKTHROUGH

Day 28

Breakthrough
The declaration of **Breakthrough** is a spiritual battering ram to any wall or hindrance the enemy has put up to keep us from moving forward in the calling and destiny Christ has placed on our lives. We stand on His Word and what He has spoken over us. We advance as we move forward into the fullness of His promises over us, our dreams, and our passions.

The enemy would love to slow us down and stop the fullness of the Kingdom of God from being established in our lives. So today, we get to systematically remove each and every hindrance in the spiritual realm. Remember, Breakthrough is not just about what we tear down, but the action of advancing.

The goal is not to stay where we are, but to break through. That requires action. Get ready for shifts and movement as you declare Breakthrough today to advance.

> The goal is not to stay where we are, but to **break through**

BREAKTHROUGH

Day 28

Today,

I declare **BREAKTHROUGH!**

I will not be hindered, stopped, limited, or diminished in this time, hour, and place in my life. I call down the supernatural and divine will of God to be manifested in my home, my family, my work, my school, my dreams, and my destiny. Like a fire shut up in my bones, I release the awesome power of the Holy Spirit to bring healing, restoration, release, and favor in my life.

I declare open doors, divine opportunities, godly relationships, friendships, and heavenly acceleration. I speak hope into areas of doubt, faith into areas of unbelief, joy into frustrations, peace into every circumstance, and patience to complete perfect work. I lay hold of every promise on my life and I contend for their fulfillment in me and my family. I am a testimony to the Greatness of a great God!

Today, I declare His Greatness will be seen as I live greatly!

"When the enemy shall come in, like a flood, the Spirit of the Lord shall raise up a standard against him." Isaiah 59:19

EXTRAVAGANT LOVE

Day 29

Extravagant Love

Love is who God is and what others will know us by. It is the very essence of our Creator. It is what motivated Christ to the cross and what couldn't keep Him in the grave. Love, His extravagant Love, is unconditional and nothing can separate us from it. His Love is not waiting for us to do something, it is right here for us.

God's Love does not require a certain response or action and does not ask anything of us: it just is. When we receive the extravagance of His Love it can transform us, renew us, and restore us. It ignites joy, releases laughter, and refreshes hearts. His Love has been pursuing you, longing for you, yearning for you. His Love wants to encounter you. The best way to release His Love is to receive His Love.

The declaration of Extravagant Love today is about choosing to receive it; allowing His Love to permeate into your heart, your mind and your soul. Take a moment today to declare it, and then simply receive the Father's Love.

God's Love does not require a certain response or action and does not ask anything of us

EXTRAVAGANT LOVE

Day29

Today,

I declare **EXTRAVAGANT LOVE!**

It cannot be stopped, hindered, reduced, or limited. It is bigger, grander, larger, more powerful, and more amazing than any mind can believe or imagine. I release the Extravagant Love of God to fill me and to move in and through my life, my family, my home, my work, my school, my dreams, and my destiny. I declare an increase of the Love of God in my relationships and my friendships. I will see through eyes of Love to increase hope; speak through Love to increase life; and hear words of Love to increase faith. Let Love abound. Where there is fear, I release an increase of Love. Where there is doubt, I release waves of Love. Where there is hurt, I release healing Love. I will not be stopped or hindered by past offenses.

I invite the Extravagant Love of God to wash over me and every situation in my life as I move forward into destiny.

Today is a great day to Love again because our great God is LOVE!

"Beloved, let us love one another, for love is from God and whoever loves has been born of God and knows God." 1 John 4:7

CREATIVITY

Day 30

Creativity

The declaration of **Creativity** releases the heartbeat of God into our lives. It breaks off the monotony of form and function, removes the cobwebs of routine, and blows off the dust of stagnation. Creativity releases a wave of inspiration and ideas. It allows the Holy Spirit to stir in the area of ingenuity and release freshness into ideas and thoughts.

> We were created in His image; and, when **He speaks, He creates**

The declaration of Creativity is also a declaration of war on religion. Religion needs rules and regulations to live and breathe. Religion needs consistency, predictability and control. Because Creativity comes alive with unbridled freshness and newness, it can create mess in its productivity. God doesn't want us to just do, He wants us to create. We were created in His image; and, when He speaks, He creates.

Today, declare Creativity in your life and come alive with newness in Him.

CREATIVITY

Day 30

Today,

I declare **CREATIVITY**!

I release supernatural, powerful, heavenly creativity and imagination over myself, my family, my work, and my school. I tap into the unlimited resource of Heaven's artistic language.

Today's problems and situations will not be hindered by yesterday's solutions. I speak new ideas, original thoughts, colorful dreams, and fresh revelation over any roadblock, creativity block, or other hindering circumstance.

I tap into a new sound, new song, new inventions, books, dances, plays, movies, and scripts. I unleash heavenly waves that allow me to see new, believe new, and experience new today.

Today will be great because I will express Greatness everywhere I go!

"In the beginning God created..." Genesis 1:1

"He put a new song in my mouth..." Psalm 40:3

GOODNESS
Day 31

Goodness

Our God is a good God. Take a moment and say that out loud. "Our God is a good God." Now believe it. Our ability to know that God is a good God transforms our identity; He is our Heavenly Father and we are cut from that same spiritual DNA. When we know that our God is a good God, it changes how we see every day events in our lives and our circumstances. Not only is God good, He has **Goodness** for us. He longs to pour out His Goodness into our lives and let our lives be a testimony of His character and His heart.

Psalm 31:19 says that God has abundant Goodness stored up for us. He longs for Goodness to be realized in our lives and seen in our families, workplace and city. His Goodness is not just for us, but so the world around us to know Him. Psalm 34:8 tell us to taste and see that the Lord is good. Romans 2:4 explains that God's Goodness leads people to repentance.

Today, your declaration of Goodness speaks both to the heart of who your Father is and to who He longs to be in your life.

"Surely Goodness and mercy shall follow me all the days of my life, and I shall dwell in the house of the Lord forever!" Psalm 23:6

GOODNESS

Day 31

Today,

I declare **GOODNESS!**

I break off any negative thoughts or words spoken over me that do not lift me up, encourage me, or cause me to walk in the fullness of who I am in Christ **Jesus. I come out of agreement with any destructive** identity or understanding of who I am. I press completely into the awesomeness of a mighty God and I find my identity in who He is. I release Goodness into my home, my family, my work, my school, my dreams, and my destiny. I declare that everything I lay my hand to will produce good fruit and bring life and joy.

The Goodness of God in me cannot be contained and will spring up in my life as a testimony to God's Greatness.

Today is a good day to be great because today I declare Greatness is GOOD!

"Oh how abundant is Your Goodness, which you have stored up for those who fear you and worked for those who take refuge in you." Psalm 31:19

SALVATION

Day 32

Salvation

The declaration of **Salvation** is so much more than just saving us from sin and death. Jesus is our Savior in life. When we face touchy situations and circumstances, it is important to know to Whom to run to and in Whom to abide. Christ did not die on the cross and rise again three days later for us to simply have life eternally, but to have life today.

When we face obstacles we believe cannot be overcome, or feel dead in our job, relationships, or battles we are facing, we can call on Jesus Christ, our Salvation.

As you declare Salvation over your life and region today, you are declaring the saving and restoring power of God.

"The name of the Lord is a strong tower; the righteous run to it and are saved." Proverbs 18:10

I have seen the battle, and **the battle is the Lord's**

SALVATION

Day 32

Today,

I declare **SALVATION!**

You, O Lord, are my refuge and my strength. You, O Lord, are my strong tower. I cry out to You in the day of my infirmity and my affliction, where war and pestilence are all around me, and I declare that you are my Salvation! I awaken my soul to the song of victory and I lift my eyes to see the help of the Lord. May faith rise up, may hope be restored, may joy rush in like a mighty river. I speak salvation over my home, my family, my work, my school, my dreams, and my destiny.

I have seen the battle, and the battle is the Lord's. I break off any fear, doubt, and worry. My God is bigger, my God is stronger, and my God has the victory! The day of the Salvation of the Lord is upon me.

Today will be a great day because Greatness belongs to my God!

"I will call upon the Lord, who is worthy to be praised; so shall I be saved from my enemies." Psalm 18:3

FAITHFULNESS

Day 33

Faithfulness

When we know that we have a faithful God; when we read in Scripture that He will never leave us or forsake us, we can actually believe it. When we hear that nothing can separate us from His love, it rings true because they are words found within His **faithful nature. God's Faithfulness gives us assurance** as we step out in faith into the unknown: the dreams and visions He has placed on our heart.

God's Faithfulness reminds us that His promises are true; He will meet every need as we do what he has called us to do. Our declaration of Faithfulness extends beyond us to our families, over our children, to our city, and our country.

Today, as you declare God's Faithfulness you are reminding yourself, and the world around you, of the Faithfulness of the God you serve who keeps His promises.

"Your love O Lord, reaches to the heavens, and your faithfulness to the skies." Psalm 36:5

FAITHFULNESS

Day 33

Today,

I declare **FAITHFULNESS**!

I release God's true and just words and promises over myself, my family, my home, my work, my school, my dreams, and my destiny. I lay hold of the unfailing assurances of a mighty and faithful God. Over sickness, I release health. Over lack, I release provision. Over fear, I release love. Over doubt, I release hope. Over frustration, I release opportunity. Over every area that does not line up as truth of a faithful God, I release the divine nature of Christ and His faithfulness.

Today, I will walk in the fullness of what God has called me to, spoken over me, and placed as a burning desire in my heart. I will release His faithful Word over the land and community around me, that all will experience the goodness of a Great God.

Today, I will experience Greatness in the Faithfulness of a Great God!

"I will sing of the Lord's great love forever; with my mouth I will make Your faithfulness know through all generations." Psalm 89:1

CHOSEN

Day 34

Chosen

So many times we are waiting to be **Chosen**, like at an Elementary school game on the blacktop. "Pick me, pick me!" The reality is in Christ we are already called. "Chosen," however, reflects our response to that call. Chosen is a decision we get to make.

In your life right now, when you decide to be "Chosen" you are agreeing to be the one to bring healing, restoration, and life into a situation. You are not waiting on some heavenly voice to call you out. Instead, you are walking in the fullness of what God has already given you. In your choice to lay hold of the spiritual gifts He has poured out for you already, you walk in the authority of who you are in Christ.

Today, by declaring you are Chosen, you step into the fullness of what it means to be "in Christ" and allow Him to be manifested in your life.

> You are a **chosen generation**, a royal priesthood, a holy nation, His own special people, called out of darkness into the glorious light to ordain His praise
> 1 Peter 2:9

CHOSEN

Day 34

Today,

I declare I am **CHOSEN**!

I have been called and chosen for such a time as this. This is my season, my hour, my opportunity, and my time. I release favor and the supernatural outpouring of Heaven over my family, my home, my work, my school, my dreams, and my destiny. I release heavenly strength to not grow weary, supernatural grace and patience, and stir hunger and desire within me to not let go of that which I have been called. I will walk as one marked and set aside for this time and this moment.

I release greater things, greater works, greater **miracles, greater healings, and greater breakthroughs** now in my life. I break off doubt, frustration, agitation, fear ,and the lies of the enemy. I release the Word of a great God in my life.

Today will be a day of Greatness because I have been Chosen to be great!

You are a chosen generation, a royal priesthood, a holy nation, His own special people, called out of darkness into the glorious light to ordain His praise!"
1 Peter 2:9"

REFRESHING

Day 35

Refreshing

It is so easy to become burned out in life, to get tired and drained from the duties of family life, work, even ministry. When we walk in what God has called us to, we are continually pouring ourselves out into others all around us. That can be draining, which is why it is so important to be continually **Refreshed** in the living water of the Holy Spirit.

Isaiah 35:6 says that God will make streams in the desert. When we are dry and thirsty or worn and **weary He is a good God who Refreshes and restores** us. He wants His river of living water to first spring up in and through us, so we can then bring refreshing to those around us.

Today, declare His Refreshing waters in your life, work, ministry, and dreams and allow those around you to be refreshed as well.

"...for waters shall burst forth in the wilderness, and streams in the desert." Isaiah 35:6

When we are dry and thirsty
**He is a good God who
Refreshes and restores us**

REFRESHING

Day 35

Today,

I declare **REFRESHING**!

I release a fresh and new outpouring of the presence of God over myself, my family, my home, my work, my school, my dreams, and my destiny. I allow the Holy Spirit to wash over me and bring Refreshing to my mind, to break off old habits, old mindsets, old addictions, old thoughts, and old functions. I declare fresh vision, fresh hope, fresh love, and fresh faith will rise up in me and overwhelm me with the goodness of God.

I invite God's mercies to restore me, His grace to renew me (and all those around me), and His goodness to bless me and allow me to be a blessing. Today, I meditate on His Words over me; I Refresh myself with His Word in me, and I release His Word to the world around me.

Today, I Refresh myself in the Greatness of my Destiny!

"Whoever believes in me, as the Scripture has said, streams of living water will flow from within him!"
John 7:38

MINE

Day 36

Mine

So often we are waiting for opportunities and special times that are just for us. We want that perfect moment. Maybe you are waiting for your time to shine. Good news – today is that day. God made this day just for you and he made you just for today. This day is full of possibilities and potential, along with its mystery and unknowns.

God created today just for you and He has equipped you with everything you need to walk in victory and greatness today. What we each need to realize is that today is **"Mine."** We are not promised tomorrow or the next day. We don't always know exactly what the future holds. However, if you woke up today, if you opened your eyes and felt breath in your lungs, then today is your day and God has great things in store.

Grab a hold of today with purpose and determination to walk in the authority that God has given you, as His own. Don't allow the enemy to have today. This day was made for you!

Day 36

Today,

I declare is **MINE**!

God, you made today wonderful and amazing and you gave it to me! Today, I will overcome, I will thrive, I will succeed, and I will be more than a conqueror. Today, I will see healings, miracles, breakthroughs, and restorations. I will see the fulfillment of promises in me, my family, my work, my school, my dreams, and my destiny. God has prepared the way, has gone before me, and He is directing and ordering my steps.

I break off any lie, attack or plan of the enemy from me or my journey. I press in fully to the love of God, the promises of God, and the embrace of God. I release the fullness of the Holy Spirit to wash over me, overwhelm me, and saturate me.

Today, I lay hold of Greatness, for today will be a great day!

"This is the day that the Lord has made; let us rejoice and be glad in it!" Psalm 118:24

ABUNDANCE

Day 37

Abundance

Our God is not a God of just enough, but a God of *more* than enough. He doesn't just meet needs, He exceeds them. He doesn't just fill a cup, He fills it to overflowing. He is a God of **Abundance**. God has Abundant joy for us, abundant love for us, and Abundant grace for us. His love, joy, and grace never runs out, never runs dry. It is continuously pouring over us.

We know that our God provides, renews, and restores. However, do you know that He does it Abundantly? Do you know He longs to show off His love and goodness in your life? Do you know you are a testimony to the Greatness of a great God?

When we declare the Abundance of God, we are releasing it into our lives and the lives of all those around us. That is called the splash zone.

Our God is a **God of more than enough**

ABUNDANCE

Day 37

Today,

I declare ABUNDANCE!

I release the overflowing goodness of Heaven to be poured out in and through my life today. All the resources and provisions for the dreams and destiny that God has called me to will be released today! I declare the Abundance of Heaven in my life, my home, my family, my school and my job. My region will flourish with the fullness of the promises of God. I release healings, miracles, restoration, and supernatural God encounters today.

Today, I embrace the Abundance of God's love, the joy of His Spirit, renewed faith, fresh hope, and greater vision. Today, I break off any lies of lack, any thoughts of less, and any poverty mindset or mentality. My God is the God of more, of Abundance, and I walk in the fullness of that.

Today, I will not just experience Greatness, today I will be great!

"Now to Him who is able to do exceedingly Abundantly above all that we ask or hope for, according to the power that works in us!"

GLORY

Day 38

Glory

God's **Glory** is the essence of who He is. It is the very beauty of His Spirit. It is not a physical reflection of what He looks like but a reflection of the character of a loving God. Hebrews 2:6-7 says He has crowned us with His Glory. The very character and essence of God is upon us. Not only do we get to bring it everywhere we go, but we get to deposit His Glory in our families, our workplace, and our region.

We were designed to be carriers of His Glory and to showcase it for all to see. Psalm 72:19 also says that the whole earth is filled with His Glory. We get to draw that out. We get to speak to that Glory and reveal it to a world that cannot see it.

A declaration of His Glory is a declaration of God to the Earth.

"...What is man that you are mindful of him, or the son of man that You take care of him? You have made him a little lower than the angels; You have crowned him with glory and honor, and set him over the works of Your hands." Hebrews 2:6-7

GLORY

Day 38

Today,

I declare the **GLORY** of the Lord!

I passionately and violently lay hold of the Heavens and bring a righteous invasion of the Glory of God to Earth. I declare that God's Glory will surround, overwhelm and fill every aspect of my life, my home, my work, my school, my dreams, and my destiny.

In His presence today, there will be miracles, healings, breakthrough, and restoration; that I may be strengthened, encouraged, and find fullness of joy. Glory will be a testimony to the Greatness and might of my God and every attack, plan, or strategy of the enemy will be broken, dismantled, and removed.

I release waves of Heaven's Glory to cover my city, **my region, my state, and my nation. The goodness and Greatness of God will overwhelm and cover this land.**

Today, God's greatness will be shown in the Greatness of His Glory on my life!

"Declare His glory among the nations, His marvelous works among all peoples." 1 Chronicles 16:24

JUSTICE

Day 39

Justice

God's **Justice** is more than just judgment over sin and death. His Justice is righting anything that is not aligned with the Kingdom of God. His Justice sets straight injustices that are taking place all around us. God's Justice of sickness is healing. God's Justice over death is life. God's Justice over sorrow is joy.

When we declare His Justice in our life, we are saying, "Lord, any area that does not line up with Your Kingdom and Your heart, please set it right." When we speak Justice over our family, we are giving Him permission to align our home with His heart.

When we speak Justice over our community, we are inviting the justice of God to bring our city, our state, and our workplace into alignment with His Kingdom, His will, and His purpose.

> When we speak **Justice** over our family, we are giving Him permission to align our home with His heart

JUSTICE

Day 39

Today,

I declare **JUSTICE**!

My God is a God that heals. My God delivers. My God goes before me. My God saves. My God is a God of righteousness. I remind my God of His Greatness and His goodness, and unleash the fullness of His Justice in my life, my family, my work, my school, my dreams, and my destiny! Today, no weapon formed against me shall prosper. I release the righteous judgments of Heaven over all sickness, disease, and any attack on my body, my family, and my region.

I release faith to believe the impossible, love to love the unlovable, hope to pursue dreams, and power to live greatly. I press into the arms of a just and loving God and allow the power of His Spirit to fill me, saturate me, and overwhelm me. Today, nothing shall stop me, slow me down, or hinder me from what my God has called me to do.

Today, watch out, because I am living greatly!

"Follow Justice and Justice alone, so that you may live and posses the land the Lord your God is giving you!" Deuteronomy 16:20

CELEBRATION

Day 40

Celebration

Celebration comes when we are awakened to the truth of who we are in God and the fullness of His promises for our lives. There is a release of incredible joy and happiness not found in circumstances or in moods. Celebration is released by the revelation of who our God is and who He wants to be to us.

God does not want us to merely live; He longs for us to have life and abundant life. He longs for us to walk in Greatness, to be over comers, and victorious in all our circumstances. He removed all sin and death so we can walk abundantly, healed, restored, powerful, and mighty. He has lavished upon us His love and equipped us with gifts. He has done this so that we can be a true light of who He is to a world that does not know Him. That is reason to celebrate.

A declaration of Celebration is a release of the fullness of God in your life and an understanding that you were made for Him.

Today, I will rejoice in the **Lord**

CELEBRATION

Day 40

Today,

I declare **CELEBRATION!**

Today, I will rejoice in the Lord. I will Celebrate who God is and what He is doing in my life, my home, my work, my school, my dreams, and my destiny. I release an overflowing of goodness and God's faithfulness.

Today, I press into His Spirit and unleash rivers of living water into every area of my life. I lay hold of His joy and His pleasure as a testimony of a great God.

Today will be a great day of Celebration because my God is doing so many great things in my life!

"You have made known to me the path of life; you will fill me with Joy in your presence, with eternal pleasures at your right hand!" Psalm 16:11

Matthew Oliver
The Family Church
1529 Eureka Road, Suite 110
Roseville, California 95661
(916) 791-7555
www.JoinTheFamily.net

50872073R10055

Made in the USA
San Bernardino, CA
06 July 2017